Desert Animals

Written by Jen Green
Illustrated by Michael Posen

DP
DEMPSEY
PARR

This edition is for Books Are Fun

This is a Dempsey Parr Book
First published in 2000

Dempsey Parr is
an imprint of Parragon
Parragon
Queen Street House
4 Queen Street
Bath BA1 1HE, UK

ISBN 1-84084-776-X

Printed in Dubai, U.A.E

Produced by
Monkey Puzzle Media Ltd
Gissing's Farm
Fressingfield
Suffolk IP21 5SH
UK

Designer: Sarah Crouch
Cover design: Victoria Webb
Editor: Linda Sonntag
Artwork commissioning:
Roger Goddard-Coote
Project manager: Alex Edmonds

Contents

Fennec foxes are the world's smallest foxes, but have the largest ears of any fox.

Fennec fox

Do many desert animals have large ears?

Fennec foxes, of the Sahara Desert, have large pointed ears. So do kit foxes of American deserts, and also desert hedgehogs. All these creatures' ears work in the same way as the jack rabbit's do. They radiate heat to keep the animal cool.

How do its ears help a jack rabbit keep cool?

Jack rabbits are desert hares with very long ears. The thin skin inside the ear is criss-crossed with delicate blood vessels. Blood flowing through the ears gives off heat, helping the animal to keep cool in scorching weather.

How do desert animals keep cool?

DESERTS ARE HOT, DRY PLACES WHERE ALMOST NO RAIN FALLS. EACH DAY, the sun beats down fiercely from cloudless skies. At first glance, deserts seem lifeless places, but in fact all kinds of creatures live there. Many desert animals spend the scorching midday hours in underground burrows. Burrow-dwellers include snakes, lizards and tortoises, rodents, and other mammals, and even some kinds of birds.

Are deserts always hot?

At night, deserts are often very cold. The temperature drops steeply in the evening because there are no clouds to keep in the day's heat. Some deserts in central Asia are cold even by day. So desert creatures must be able to cope with cold, as well as heat. Dwarf hamsters, of Mongolia, have thick fur, which they fluff out to keep warm at night. Bactrian camels grow thick fur for the winter, and molt again in spring.

Do desert creatures ever sleep for long periods?

Some desert creatures, such as tortoises, enter a deep sleep called aestivation to avoid the hottest summer weather. In harsh Mongolian deserts, furry mammals called susliks sleep out the scorching summer; they also hibernate in winter. Aestivation comes from the Latin word for summer, and hibernation from the Latin word for winter.

When do desert creatures go hunting?

By day, the weather is too hot for most desert animals to hunt. Foxes, and other predators (hunters), rest in their cool burrows. They emerge as night falls, and hunt in the cool of darkness.

Which desert creature has a built-in sunshade?

Ground squirrels, of American and South African deserts, have long, bushy tails. When searching for food in the hot sun, the squirrel fluffs out its tail and holds it over its head, to act as a shady parasol.

How do cold-blooded creatures cope with the heat?

SNAKES, LIZARDS AND MANY OTHER REPTILES LIVE IN DESERTS. REPTILES are cold-blooded creatures – their body temperature is not controlled by a thermostat in their body like ours is, but by their surroundings. Throughout the day, they change their position to regulate their temperature so they can stay active. A desert lizard basks in the sun in the early morning to warm up. When the sun blazes down at midday, it moves into the shade to cool off. It sunbathes again in the evening so its body stays warm at night.

Ground squirrel

Ground squirrels use their tails to shade themselves from the baking sun. In the very hottest weather they retreat to their underground burrows.

What stands on its head to drink fog?

Darkling beetles live in the Namib desert, near the coast of

South-west Africa. This desert is often covered in sea fog. When the weather is foggy, the beetle emerges from its burrow and does a headstand, so its rear end points in the air. Moisture from the fog condenses on the beetle's body and trickles down into its mouth.

The darkling beetle stands on its head to drink in the Namib Desert.

Darkling beetle

What is the thirstiest desert creature?
Camels are well-known desert survivors. They can last for days without water – weeks if they have plants to eat. At waterholes and wells, camels "refuel" by drinking huge quantities of water quickly. A thirsty camel can gulp down 22 gallons (100 litres) in just a few minutes!

What stores its food in its tail?
Gila monsters are plump lizards of Californian deserts. The reptile's fat tail acts as an emergency food store in dry weather. Its body converts the fat in its tail into energy and slims down when food is scarce.

Why don't camels get sunburn?
A camel's whole body is suited to desert-dwelling. Long, coarse hair on the animal's head, neck, and back protects its skin from the fierce rays of the sun.

What spends 10 months underground?
Frogs and toads are water-loving creatures. You may be surprised to hear that some kinds live in deserts, too. In American deserts, spadefoot toads spend 10 months of the year hidden in deep burrows. They emerge only during the short rainy season.

What drinks the juice of a poisonous cactus?
In American deserts, pack rats eat the fruit and flesh of the saguaro cactus. They get the moisture they need from the juicy flesh, but must be careful not to munch the sharp spines! Saguaro cactus flesh contains a poison, that stops most animals from eating it, but it doesn't harm the pack rats' strong stomachs.

Why is dew the devil's favourite drink?

The thorny devil is a lizard of American deserts. Its body is covered with sharp spines that protect it from enemies. The spines also act as a water-catchment system. On cold nights dew condenses on the animal's body. Moisture runs down grooves in the spines straight into the lizard's mouth.

The thorny devil drinks dew channeled by its spines.

Which frog is its own water bag?

Water-holding frogs live in pools in Australian deserts. As the dry season approaches and the pool dries up, the frog absorbs water, which it stores under its skin. Its whole body swells until it is completely bloated. Then it burrows into the mud, to survive the drought, and only emerges again when the next rain falls.

What do animals drink in the desert?

DESERTS ARE PLACES WHERE WATER IS ALWAYS SCARCE. SOMETIMES NO rain falls for months, or even years. Desert creatures can get by on little or no water. Some types of desert antelopes, such as addax antelopes, almost never drink. They get all the moisture they need from eating grass.

Australian Aborigines sometimes dig up water-holding frogs and drink from them.

Water-holding frog

Kangaroo rats live in North American deserts.

When is a kangaroo really a rat?

Kangaroo rats have strong, springy hind legs shaped like a kangaroo's legs. As they bound along at high speed, their paws make little contact with the burning ground. These rodents also leap high in the air, to reach the young, tasty shoots of desert shrubs. Jerboas, of African and Asian deserts, are rodents with very similar hind legs that live in the same way.

Kangaroo rat

Golden moles leave tell-tale ridges of sand on the surface, as they burrow underground.

Which golden mammal "swims" through sand?

THE GOLDEN MOLE LIVES IN SOUTH Africa. Its forelegs have large, flat claws that help it to shovel sand aside, as it burrows under the surface. Its digging action is like a swimmer's breast-stroke. This little beast can dig a tunnel 2.5 miles (4 km) long in a single night.

Golden mole

Which lizard dances to cool off?

MOST LIZARDS USE ALL FOUR LEGS FOR RUNNING. THE BEARDED LIZARD of Australian deserts is different – it runs on its hind legs to keep its body off the sand. When standing still, it cools its feet by "dancing" – lifting each of its legs in turn.

Which lizard moves like a fish?

Sandfish are African lizards with long, slender bodies, like eels. They move through the sand by thrashing their body from side to side, like a fish swimming in water. The sandfish's feet have scaly fringes that can help it run along the sand.

What wears snow-shoes with hairy soles?

Desert animals, such as camels and addax antelopes, have very broad feet. Their feet act like snow-shoes, spreading the animal's weight over a wide area, to stop it sinking into soft sand. Hot sand can scorch tender animal feet, so the camel's feet have tough soles to protect them. Some other desert beasts, such as sand cats and gerbils, have feet with hairy soles for the same reason.

Which huge desert birds are champion runners?

Ostriches live in deserts and dry grasslands in Africa. These large, heavy birds can't fly, but they have very powerful legs and can race along at speeds of up to 45 mph (72 kph). They are the fastest creatures on two legs!

What young insects like to hop about in bands?

Locusts are desert insects with long hind legs and powerful muscles. Adult locusts can leap up to 10 times their own body length and can also fly. Young locusts are called hoppers. They can't fly, as their wings haven't yet developed, but they are expert jumpers. They gather in groups called bands and hop about the desert. The bigger the group, the faster these young insects hop!

Which desert animal has webbed feet?

Most animals with webbed feet live near water. The web-footed gecko lives in the Namib Desert, in southern Africa. Its webbed feet help it to run on fine sand without sinking in.

What gets there in the end?

Tortoises are slow but steady movers. Their short feet have long claws that grip on to rocks, as these armored creatures haul themselves along. The tortoise's claws also help it to dig burrows.

Why should you steer clear of a skunk doing a handstand?

In North American deserts, skunks defend themselves by spraying foul-smelling liquid at their enemies. The stinking fluid comes from scent glands under the animal's tail, so it does a handstand to aim at victims. Wise intruders back away quickly before the skunk has the chance to strike. Enemies do well to get out of range as quickly as possible.

Skunks aim a jet of foul spray at their victim's heads.

What has poisonous teeth on hinges?

Desert rattlesnakes are armed with sharp, pointed fangs. These teeth are hollow and supplied with poison, from glands in the animal's head. The rattlesnake's fangs are mounted on hinges. Normally they fold back inside its mouth, but swing forward when the snake is about to strike.

Skunk

Lanner falcon

What desert minibeasts are deadly?

Scorpions are small armored creatures distantly related to spiders. They are armed with a venomous sting that curls over their back. The sting is a sharp spine connected to a poison gland at the base of the tail. Most scorpions' stings are no more dangerous than a wasp sting, but some are armed with poison strong enough to kill a person.

Falcons usually have pointed wings and a notch in the top of their beaks.

When does a scorpion use its sting?

Scorpions use their stings mainly in self-defence, against enemies that might attack them. Only rarely do they sting their own prey – insects, mice, and lizards. Scorpions usually kill their prey by crushing them in their powerful pincer-like claws, but if a victim puts up a fierce fight, the scorpion will use its sting to paralyze it.

What desert cat is a deadly hunter?

The caracal is a fast, powerful cat from African and Asian deserts. This strong, agile hunter has large paws that can deliver a mighty blow. The caracal also has sharp claws and fierce canine teeth, to rip its victims' flesh.

What is the gila monster's secret weapon?

The North American gila monster is one of only two lizards in the world with a poisonous bite. It kills its victims by injecting them with poisonous saliva. The creature's bite is not deadly to humans, but it can be very painful.

What is green and covered in poisonous warts?

Green toads of East Africa have poison glands behind their eyes, and also poisonous warts all over their bodies. The warts produce a horrible-tasting fluid, and will put off any predator that has ever tried to eat the toad.

What desert birds are armed and dangerous?

Lanner falcons, of the Sahara Desert, are fierce birds of prey. They have strong feet with razor-sharp claws called talons, and a deadly hooked beak, to tear prey animals apart.

How do rattlesnakes warn off their enemies?

The rattlesnake gets its name from the "rattle" of loose scales on its tail. It shakes its tail to produce a loud, hissing rattle. Enemies recognize the warning and beat a hasty retreat.

Which dog steals a big cat's dinner?

Jackals live in the deserts and grasslands of Africa. They hunt in packs and scavenge whatever food they can find. Small mammals, reptiles, birds, and fruit are all on the jackal's menu. They also steal meat from kills made by other hunters, such as lions, using clever teamwork to fool the lion. One jackal distracts the hunter, while another sneaks up and pulls the meat away.

Caracals leap as high as 6.5 ft (2 metres) in the air to capture flying birds.

Caracal

Why does the jumping rodent fear the snake?

Jerboas are jumping rodents, of African and Asian deserts. They live in underground burrows where they are safe from most predators. But snakes have long, slender bodies — just the right shape to slither down the jerboas' burrows. The snake is the little rodent's most deadly enemy.

What squeezes its prey to death?

King snakes, of the American deserts, do not have a poisonous bite. Instead, they kill their prey by constriction. The snake wraps its body around a victim, such as a rat, and squeezes tighter and tighter. The victim cannot breathe, and soon dies of suffocation.

Which cat can snatch an eagle from the air?

THE CARACAL HUNTS BIRDS, ANTELOPE, MICE, AND LIZARDS. IT CAN PUT ON A burst of speed to overtake a racing antelope, and can also leap high in the air to catch desert birds. This fierce cat can kill even a large bird, like an eagle, with one swipe of its powerful paw.

What hunts with built-in heat sensors?

In American deserts, rattlesnakes can hunt prey, such as kangaroo rats, even in total darkness. Special pits near the snake's eyes are sensitive to heat and can detect the warmth of the rodent's body. The snake homes in on its prey and slithers up for the kill.

How does the rattlesnake kill its prey?

A striking rattlesnake sinks its poison fangs into its victim. Then it lets the animal go. The rat runs off, but is soon overcome by the snake's venom, and drops to the ground. The rattlesnake catches up and swallows its victim whole.

Why are waterholes dangerous?

Hungry lanner falcons hunt by lurking at waterholes. When birds, such as sandgrouse, fly in to drink at the pool, the falcon pounces and seizes a victim in its talons.

The cheetah is the fastest animal in the world.

Why does the ant lion bury itself in a pit?

STRANGE CREATURES CALLED ANT LIONS ARE THE YOUNG OF desert insects that look like dragonflies. The ant lion is a cunning hunter. It digs a small funnel-shaped pit in the sand, then buries itself in the bottom, and lies in wait. When a victim, such as an ant, falls into the pit, the ant lion pounces, and grabs its prey in its powerful jaws.

Ant lion

What is the fastest animal in the world?

Cheetahs live in dry grasslands in Africa. These sleek, lithe cats can race along at speeds of up to 62 mph (100 kph) to outrun fast prey such as gazelles.

Cheetah

What makes the kangaroo rat jump?

KANGAROO RATS LEAP HIGH IN THE AIR TO AVOID ENEMIES, SUCH AS SNAKES and foxes. Their darting leaps confuse the predator, and they may also kick sand in its face, before racing away.

What jams itself in a crack?

Chuckwalla lizards live in deserts, in the western United States. If danger threatens, the lizard speeds into a crack in the rock, then fills its body with air so it swells up. It jams itself into the crevice so a predator, such as a kit fox, cannot pull it out.

What is the domino beetle's secret weapon?

The domino ground beetle has a secret weapon. It can produce a jet of burning chemicals from its abdomen (rear end), which it squirts in the face of enemies, to ward off attack.

When does an owl sound like a snake?

Burrowing owls of American deserts are talented mimics. They can make a hissing, rattling noise that sounds like an angry rattlesnake. The noise frightens away most predators trying to enter the owl's burrow.

What loses its tail to save its life?

A web-footed gecko's tail helps it to balance when running, but it is not vital to the creature's survival. If a hunting bird seizes the tail, it breaks off at a special point, and the gecko escapes. Its muscles contract to stop the bleeding. In time, a new tail grows from the stump.

Desert hedgehog

What wears armor in the desert?

The desert tortoise moves far too slowly to outrun its enemies. Instead, it has an armor-plated shell, made up of many bony plates fused together. When it is threatened, the reptile pulls its head and limbs inside the shell so a hunter cannot reach the soft parts of its body.

Desert tortoise

The tortoise's shell stops it from drying out.

A fox attempting to attack a desert hedgehog will end up with a mouthful of prickles.

Which snake pretends to be dead?

Hognose snakes are non-venomous snakes from the western United States and Mexico. The snake hisses loudly to frighten away attackers. If this does not work the hognose plays dead, rolling on to its back and lying still, with its mouth open and its tongue lolling out. Many predators will not touch dead prey, so the snake's plan often works well.

What puts up its hood and spits poison?

The RED COBRA IS A POISONOUS SNAKE THAT LURKS BY waterholes in East Africa. When danger threatens, the cobra raises the skin round its neck to make a threatening hood. If an intruder, such as a person, does not back away, the snake spits poison into its victim's eyes. Humans, who've been attacked, can go blind if their eyes are not treated quickly.

Why might a fox get a mouthful of prickles?

Desert hedgehogs live in North Africa and Arabia. If a predator, such as a fennec fox, attacks, the hedgehog curls up into a ball. Tough spines protect its back, and the fox cannot reach its head and soft belly.

How did the domino beetle get its name?

The domino beetle is so-called because the white spots on its black body make it look like a domino. This coloration also acts as a warning signal, showing that the beetle is armed with poisonous chemicals. Predators that have been sprayed with poison once will avoid these beetles in future.

Vibrant markings, like those on the domino beetle, show that a creature is poisonous.

Domino beetle

Predators looking at the "two heads" of the shingleback lizard don't know which end might bite back.

Shingleback lizard

Why does the sand cat seem invisible?

THE SAND CAT'S FUR IS BROWNY-YELLOW IN COLOR, WITH DARK markings on its head, legs, and tail. These subtle colors and patterns, known as camouflage, blend in with its surroundings, so the cat can hunt without being seen. It stalks prey, such as jerboas, by approaching stealthily with its body flattened against the rocks, until it is close enough to pounce. The sand cat lives in African and Asian deserts.

Which creature seems to have two heads?

The Australian shingleback lizard has a short, plump tail that acts as a fat store. The tail also provides good camouflage, to confuse predators. It looks very like the lizard's stumpy head, so enemies don't know which end to attack.

When does a squirrel look like an antelope?

Antelope squirrels, of American deserts, use camouflage to hide from their enemies. The squirrel has mainly brown fur, with a white stripe, like an antelope's, running down its body. The stripe helps to break up its outline, making it hard for enemies to spot. If danger threatens, the squirrel freezes and becomes almost invisible against the rocks and sand.

Which snake waits in the sand for its dinner?

The sand viper, of North African and Arabian deserts, is light brown in color. The snake hunts by lying in wait for passing lizards, and other small creatures. It chooses a spot where it can wriggle down into the loose sand. More sand blows over its body and soon only the head and watchful eyes can be seen. The viper's perfect disguise has an added advantage: it is also cooler under the desert sand.

When is a gerbil relieved to lose its tail?

Gerbils are mainly sandy-colored, so they blend in well with the Mongolian desert. But the rodent has a tuft of dark hair on its tail. If a predator, such as a fox, spots the creature moving, it will attack the dark tail end, which is easier to see than the head. If the fox manages to grab the gerbil's tail it can break off, giving the animal a chance to escape, though its tail will not grow again.

Why is the king snake orange and black?

THE KING SNAKE OF AMERICAN DESERTS IS NOT POISONOUS. BUT ITS ORANGE-and-black stripes mimic the colors of the deadly coral snake, of the same region. Enemies are fooled by its disguise and will not go near it, thinking it is a coral snake.

Why would a lizard put up an umbrella?

The Australian frilled lizard has a loose flap of skin around its neck. This frill is supported by stiff rods like those in an umbrella. When the lizard is threatened it can raise its ruff to look like a fierce and much larger creature. If this trick doesn't work, the lizard may charge and bite.

What colors warn that the gila monster is poisonous?

The poisonous gila monster lizard has orange-and-black stripes on its scaly skin. These colors are common to poisonous creatures all over the world, so they act as a warning sign that the creature is dangerous. Other animals recognize the colors and know to avoid the lizard.

Which insects do desert people fear the most?

Locusts are large grasshoppers found in African and Asian deserts. When their plant food is plentiful, they breed quickly, and gather in huge groups called swarms. A locust swarm may contain many millions of insects; as it flies off in search of food, it turns the sky black. Farmers fear these insects, because a giant swarm can destroy many acres of carefully tended crops in minutes, causing whole villages to go hungry.

Why is there safety in numbers?

Oryx are large antelope that live in herds in African and Arabian deserts. The herd provides safety in numbers because a hunter, such as a big cat, will find it difficult to target a single victim in a great herd. The oryx usually canter off to escape from danger, but if these beasts are cornered, they defend themselves with their horns.

Oryx

How do harvester ants work together?

Harvester ants nest in a large colony with a single queen. Most of the group are workers, with different jobs to do. Scout ants search out new sources of seeds, the colony's food. Other workers carry the seeds back to the nest, where soldier ants, with huge jaws, crack them open. The juicy nut kernels are carried inside the nest, and stored in special chambers, leaving a huge pile of husks outside.

An oryx lowers its head and threatens its attackers with its curved horns.

What birds run after clouds?

EMUS LIVE IN FLOCKS IN DRY PARTS OF AUSTRALIA. THESE GIANT BIRDS FEED on plants, fruit, insects, and lizards. They cannot fly, but roam the land on foot looking for food. Farmers build long stretches of tall fences, to prevent emus from destroying their crops. In times of drought, emus watch for rain clouds and run after them, in search of places where rain has fallen.

Which creature gives instructions in scent?

Naked mole rats are strange, blind mammals that live in underground burrows in Africa. The colony is ruled by a female, called the queen, who alone gives birth to young. She communicates with the other mole rats by giving off special scent signals, known as pheromones, which tell the group what to do.

Budgerigars live in flocks in the Australian outback. They have no fixed home, but fly on continually in search of areas where rain has fallen, and plants are producing seeds, their favourite food. When seeds are plentiful, the budgies take their chance to settle temporarily, make nests, and rear their young.

The budgerigar is a member of the parakeet family.

Budgerigar

Meerkat guards bark to warn the rest of the colony if an enemy approaches.

Why does a meerkat stand on its hind legs?

MANY DIFFERENT DESERT ANIMALS LIVE IN GROUPS. MEERKATS ARE furry mammals that live in a network of underground tunnels called a colony. These animals co-operate so they can feed safely above ground. One meerkat stands up on its hind legs and keeps a sharp eye out for enemies, such as snakes and hawks, while the rest feed. If the sentry spots a predator, it gives a warning bark and the group quickly disappears.

Meerkat group

Where do gerbils store their food?

When the gerbil finds a good food source, its stuffs the pouches in its cheeks with seeds. Then it returns to the safety of its burrow, to feast in peace.,

Which desert mammal is a speedy mover?

Jack rabbits of North American deserts are champion racers. They can speed along at up to 35 mph (55 kph), to outdistance predators, such as foxes.

How does the kit fox find its food?

The kit fox feeds on insects, lizards, mice and rabbits. At night, when it goes hunting, its vision is little help to track down food, but its large ears pick up the tiniest noises that betray the presence of scurrying prey. The kit fox is also known as the swift fox, because it can run very fast.

How do echidnas eat their meals?

The echidna, or spiny anteater, is an unusual mammal found in the Australian outback. It feeds on insects and termites, which it slurps up with its long, sticky tongue.

What makes its nest in a cactus bush?

PACK RATS BUILD THEIR NESTS IN CACTUS BUSHES IN NORTH American deserts. They pile more cacti up around the nest to deter predators, such as foxes, and leave only a tiny entrance hole so the fox cannot get in. The nest contains several cool, comfy chambers, where the pack rats sleep by day.

Gerbil

What desert beast is known for its bad temper?

Camels are well known for their bad temper and unpredictable behavior. They may savagely bite, or kick anyone, who annoys them, or spit foul-smelling liquid. At night, their owners have to hobble them (tie their legs together) to stop them escaping back to the wild.

What is a camel's hump made of?

A camel's hump does not contain water, as some people think. In fact, it is a store of fat, which the animal can live off when food is scarce. An Arabian camel's hump shrinks, as the fat inside is used up in hard times. A bactrian camel's humps flop over.

Camels

The two-humped bactrian and one-humped dromedary camel.

How many humps do camels have?

THERE ARE TWO DIFFERENT TYPES OF CAMEL. ARABIAN CAMELS (DROMEDARIES) HAVE a single hump. They are found in North Africa as well as Arabia. Bactrian camels come from the Gobi Desert and other dry parts of Asia. These hairy beasts have not one hump, but two.

Gerbils are desert rodents that feed mainly on seeds.

Why is the camel called the ship of the desert?

Camels are strong, hardy beasts that have been domesticated (tamed) for thousands of years. Before the days of trucks and planes, they were used to ferry heavy loads across the desert, where the huge sand dunes often look like waves. Camels are also used as riding animals, but their rolling walk gives a bumpy ride, rather like a boat in a choppy sea. It makes some riders "seasick"!

Why don't camels get sand up their noses and in their eyes?

Windy deserts are no problem for camels. Their nostrils close between breaths to keep the sand out, and long eyelashes protect their eyes from blowing sand. In sandstorms they shut their eyes, but can see well enough through their thin eyelids to keep moving, if necessary.

Gila woodpecker

Which bird makes a hole in a cactus to nest in?

Woodpeckers normally nest in trees, but there are few trees in the desert. The gila woodpecker, of American deserts nests in the tall saguaro cactus instead. It drills out its nest hole with its strong, sharp beak. In time, the juicy flesh, inside the hole, dries out to make a cool, safe place for the bird to raise its chicks.

Gila woodpeckers chisel out their home with their powerful beaks.

What desert bird has a secondhand home?

The elf owl takes over the nest hole drilled by gila woodpeckers, once the woodpeckers have left. It rests in its secondhand home by day, and goes out at night to hunt insects, spiders, and small lizards.

Which bird lives in a burrow?

THE BURROWING OWL MAKES ITS HOME UNDERGROUND. IT CAN dig out its own nest burrow with its sharp beak and claws, but the bird is naturally lazy: it prefers to take over an abandoned ground squirrel burrow, if it can.

Why don't vultures get thirsty?

VULTURES ARE SCAVENGERS: THEY FEED ON THE CARCASSES OF DEAD creatures. These large birds get all the liquid they need, from the blood and flesh of the beasts on which they feed. In deserts, they soar high in the air to keep cool.

Which American bird is a speedy runner?
The roadrunner, from the North American West races along the ground at speeds of up to 40 mph (67 kph). The bird puts on a burst of speed to overtake its prey. It uses its short wings to balance, and its long tail as a rudder, to help it swerve and steer.

Roadrunner

How do roadrunners kill their prey?
The roadrunner feeds on insects, rodents, birds, and even fierce lizards and snakes. It kills its prey with one peck of its vicious beak, or crushes its victim with its powerful feet.

Which bird builds a nest on top of a cactus?
The cactus wren nests in the saguaro cactus. It builds a large domed nest high on the cactus, where the rows of sharp spines put off any hunters, that might prey on the nestlings. The wren's tough feathers and scaly legs protect it from the spines.

How did roadrunners get their name?
In the days of the American pioneers, roadrunners were named for their habit of running along desert tracks, behind the wagon trains. The birds followed the wagons to catch insects, disturbed by the cartwheels and the horses' hooves.

How did the mourning dove get its name?
The mourning dove lives in the deserts and plains of North America. It is named for the sad, cooing sound it makes. This dove can survive in the hottest parts of the desert, but must drink regularly. It will fly up to 60 miles (100 km) each day to find water.

Roadrunners are weak fliers but fast runners.

In Australia, Aborigines eat honeypot ants like sweets.

Honeypot ants

How do honey pot ants get their name?

Honeypot ants that feed on flower nectar run low on food in the long dry season. But they have a clever way of storing food. When flowers are plentiful, they feed the nectar to special ants called repletes. The bodies of these ants swell up so they become living honey stores (or honeypots). The repletes feed the other ants, when food is scarce.

Why do honeypot ants take other insects prisoner?

Honeypot ants live in a colony. Most kinds feed on nectar from flowers, but some get their food in an amazing way. They capture aphids, or cochineal insects, and keep them captive in their nest. The ants stroke their prisoners with their antennae (feelers), to make the insects produce honeydew, a sweet liquid, for the colony to drink.

Why does a scorpion have hairy legs?

Scorpions have poor eyesight, but a keen sense of touch and smell. Their legs are covered with tiny sensitive bristles. The little hairs can detect vibrations caused by other creatures' movements. The scorpion can tell the size of its prey from the signals it receives.

How do scorpions eat mice and lizards?

Scorpions catch quite large prey, such as mice and lizards, but they only have tiny mouths. They smother their prey in digestive juices. Their powerful pincers help pull the animal apart, and crush it to a crunchy mush, which the scorpion sucks into its mouth.

How does the jewel wasp feed its young?

WHEN THE JEWEL WASP IS READY TO LAY ITS EGGS, IT DIGS A BURROW and then goes hunting. It catches a cockroach and paralyzes it with its sting. Then it drags its victim back to the burrow, and lays an egg on it. When the wasp larva hatches out, it enjoys live cockroach meat.

How does the jewel wasp get its name?

The jewel wasp, of western America, is named for the bright metallic colors on its body case, which make it look like a gleaming jewel.

A female jewel wasp drags a victim back to her nest. Her young are legless, because they do not need to move to find their food.

Jewel wasp

How do trapdoor spiders get their name?

The trapdoor spider, which lives in western America, sets a clever trap for its prey. It digs a burrow and lines it with silk, from its abdomen. Then it fashions a little lid from earth and silk, and attaches it to the top with a silken hinge. It lurks just inside its burrow. When an insect passes, the spider flips its lid and leaps out to grab its meal.

What insects do people like to eat?

Young insects called wichetty grubs are a favorite food of Australian Aborigines. These grubs live underground on tree roots. Aborigines dig them up and eat them raw or cooked. In African deserts, people also eat grasshoppers and other insects.

Which spider eats until it drops?

Camel spiders of African deserts are greedy hunters. They can eat as many as 100 insects in a day, and sometimes get so full they can hardly walk. The camel spider hunts at night, and before it has eaten it can move very quickly. Its front legs have special suckers, so it can run straight up smooth walls, to grab lizards and even small birds in its powerful jaws.

Sand viper

What uses its eyeballs to help it swallow?

T HE GREEN TOAD CATCHES INSECTS AND OTHER MINIBEASTS WITH ITS

long, sticky tongue. As it has no teeth, the toad can't chew, and must swallow its prey whole. As it swallows, its eyeballs sink down into its mouth, to help force the food down its throat.

The green toad has an effective green camouflage.

The sand viper takes many days to digest a large meal.

How do snakes swallow creatures bigger than themselves?

Desert snakes hunt largish prey, such as rats and ground squirrels. They do not chew their food, but swallow it whole. Their jaws are very flexible with a double hinge, so the reptile can open its mouth very wide, and swallow prey larger than its own head.

Green toad

26

How can you tell a rattlesnake's age?
A rattlesnake's rattle is made up of loose rings of hard scales. A new ring is added to the rattle each time the snake sheds its skin, so the oldest snakes often have the loudest rattles.

Which invisible creature hunts with its tongue?
The chameleon is a true camouflage expert. This lizard can change the color of its skin, to match its surroundings, and so sneak up on insect prey. When the chameleon gets close, it shoots out its long, sticky-tipped tongue to catch its victim.

What lizard spends most of its life asleep?
The chuckwalla lizard is up and about in spring and early summer, when the desert flowers are blooming. It spends its waking days feeding on flowers, but sleeps for seven months of the year when the weather is harsh, and there is little food to eat.

What beats off enemies with its tail?
The spiny-tailed agama is a lizard, from the Sahara Desert, with a fat, scaly tail. If an enemy approaches, the agama runs into its burrow head-first, but leaves its tail sticking out. The armored tail swishes furiously from side to side, to ward off attack.

Do desert tortoises eat fast food?
No! The tortoise is too slow to catch active prey, but it is an all-round feeder. It eats green plants, flowers, and also dung and dead animals — in fact, most things that can't run away!

As it slithers sideways, only a small part of the sidewinder's body touches the burning sand.

What smells with its tongue?

SNAKES CAN'T HEAR OR SEE WELL ENOUGH TO HUNT THEIR PREY,
but they can sense vibrations in the ground, and they have an excellent sense of smell. Tiny scent particles in the air are collected by the snake's flickering tongue. They are transferred to a special scent-detecting organ, called the Jacobson's organ, found in the roof of the snake's mouth.

Which snake moves sideways?
Sidewinder snakes, of North America, are so-called because they move by looping their body and slithering sideways. Scales on the underside of the snake's body grip the sand. As it passes, the sidewinder leaves a line of parallel tracks across the desert.

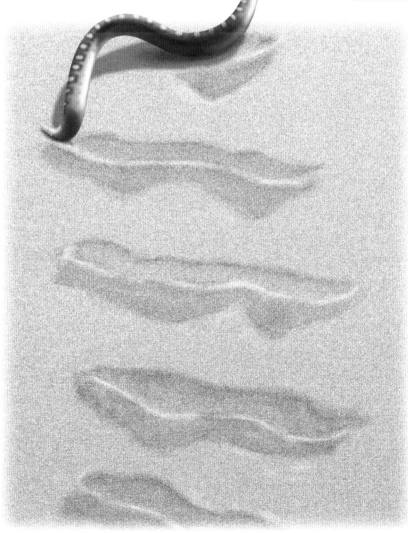

Sidewinder

What desert bird is always faithful?

Galahs are from Australia, with pink breast feathers. These pretty birds pair up for life, and return, each year, to the same nest hole in a tree. They feed their chicks on seeds, and change their breeding habits according to desert conditions. If rain has fallen, and there is plenty of food, they raise up to five chicks. In times of drought, they raise only one chick, or none at all.

Galah

Galahs are members of the cockatoo family.

How do dung beetles get their name?

THE FEMALE DUNG BEETLE GOES TO A LOT of trouble to feed her babies. She finds a pile of animal dung, and molds some into a ball. Then she rolls her ball to a good spot, lays an egg in it, and buries it in the ground. When the young insect hatches out, it feeds on the dung.

How do green toads croak?

After a rainstorm, male green toads croak to attract their partners. The male produces the sound, by pumping air through vocal cords in his throat. The croaks are amplified (made louder) as they pass through air sacs in the toad's throat, which blow up like balloons.

How do great bustards dress to impress?

Great bustards are large birds of Asian deserts. In the breeding season, the male puts on a spectacular display to win a mate. He fluffs out his neck feathers, raises his tail to reveal white underfeathers, and spreads his wings to make two dazzling white fans. Then he struts about proudly. If the female is impressed, she will mate with him.

What has a tooth on its snout?

After mating, the female tortoise digs a hole in the sand, and buries her eggs there. When the young are fully developed, they break out of the shells, using a hard "tooth" on their snouts. Young tortoises have many enemies, including hawks and falcons. Most do not survive to reach adulthood.

Which male gazelle has a harem of females?

Dorcas gazelles are small, delicate deer from North African and Arabian deserts. The male has a small herd of females called a harem. He locks horns with rival males, and fights off challenges, for the right to mate with the females. After mating, the female gazelles often give birth to twins.

What gets eaten if it doesn't dance well?

Before mating, scorpions court by performing a jerky "dance" together. They clasp their front pincers, and hop up and down on the desert floor. Females may kill and eat their partners after mating, if the males don't dance well.

How do locusts make music?

The male locust makes a loud chirping sound to attract a female. He rubs a row of pegs, on each hind leg, against stiff veins on his wings, to produce the grating sound. After mating, the female locust lays her eggs in the sand.

Which desert mammal lays eggs?

THE ECHIDNA, OR SPINY ANTEATER, HAS VERY UNUSUAL BREEDING HABITS. IT is one of only two kinds of mammals, in the world, that lay eggs. The other is the duck-billed platypus.

The female echidna keeps her eggs in a special pouch in her body.

Echidna

What do budgies feed their young?

ONLY MAMMALS PRODUCE REAL MILK FOR THEIR BABIES, BUT BUDGIES FEED their chicks on a pale fluid known as "budgie milk." The females make this nutritious liquid in their throats, and feed it to their babies with their beaks. After about a month, the young budgies are strong enough to fly, and leave the nest.

Which creature hatches in two days and grows up in two weeks?

Spadefoot toads spend most of the year buried in the mud. When rain falls, they emerge and breed quickly, before the pool dries up again. The females lay their eggs in the water, and the tadpoles hatch after only two days. Most tadpoles take months to grow up, but spadefoot tadpoles become adults in just two weeks. As the pool dries out and turns to mud, the young toads bury themselves, to wait for the next shower of rain.

Emus

An emu chick sheltering from the sun beneath its father's large body.

What large birds make caring fathers?

Female emus lay their eggs in the male birds' nests, and the father sits on the eggs to incubate them. When the chicks hatch out, they follow their father for 18 months.

Which desert beast rears its young in a pouch?

Marsupials are a group of mammals that rear their young in a pouch. Marsupial moles live underground in Australian deserts. The mother's pouch opens backward, towards the tail, so sand does not smother the baby as she burrows along.

Marsupial mole

Marsupial moles spend most of their lives underground, and have very poor vision.

Which chick drinks from its father's feathers?

Sandgrouse are birds of South African deserts. They fly a long way to drink water daily. The male bird also visits the waterhole to bring water to his thirsty chicks. He wades in and soaks up water with his fluffy breast feathers. When he flies back to the nest, the chicks drink from his soggy feathers.

What happens to ant lions when they grow up?

Ant lions are young, wingless insects with fat bodies. The adult insects are long, delicate winged creatures like dragonflies. When the ant lion is fully grown it changes into a pupa (chrysalis). As it rests inside the hard pupa case, its body is transformed. Eventually, the case splits open and a beautiful winged insect climbs out.

Which insect sheds many skins?

Like other insects, hoppers have a hard outer skin. This tough layer provides good protection, but there is no space inside to grow. The young insect must molt (shed its skin) many times as it grows bigger, until it gradually reaches its adult form.

Which animal mothers employ a nanny?

Young meerkats are born in the safety of the underground colony. Like all mammals, they feed on their mother's milk. Female meerkats, known as "nannies," look after the babies when their mothers go off to feed.

How do scorpions look after their young?

MOST MINIBEASTS TAKE LITTLE CARE OF THEIR YOUNG, BUT FEMALE SCORPIONS are protective mothers. The young ride round on their mother's back, safe beneath her sting. After three weeks they are strong enough to drop off and fend for themselves.

Index